VI

Angus Council

www.angus.gov.uk/libraries

Return to.. Library

Please return/renew this item by the last date shown
Items may also be renewed by phone or online

BORDER DEFENCE

Tony Hyland

FRANKLIN WATTS

LONDON·SYDNEY

First published in 2010 by
Franklin Watts
338 Euston Road
London NW1 3BH

Franklin Watts Australia
Level 17/207 Kent Street
Sydney NSW 2000

Series editor: Adrian Cole
Art director: Jonathan Hair
Design: Simon Borrough
Picture research: Luped

Acknowledgements:
Aaron Favila / AP / Press Association Images: 11; Alamy / David R. Frazier Photolibrary, Inc.: Front Cover;
Alex Brandon / AP / Press Association Images: 15tr; Alex Grimm / Reuters: 29; Australian Customs Service
/ Getty Images: 34b; Brian Pamphilon / iStockphoto: 37b; Caro / Alamy: 41b; Charles Csavossy / U.S.
Department of Homeland Security: 24b; Courtesy of the Serious Organised Crime Agency: 18; Denis Poroy /
AP / Press Association Images: 9b; Dita Alangkara / AP / Press Association Images: 16b; Gerald L Nino / U.S.
Department of Homeland Security: 6b; Gerald L Nino / U.S. Department of Homeland Security: 7cl, 8cl, 10b,
17b, 21t, 23t, 32b, 33r; Ho New / Reuters: 38t; James Tourtellotte / U.S. Department of Homeland Security:
12t, 13t, 14b, 15tl, 17t, 20b, 21b, 22t, 23b, 26b, 27, 33l; Karim Sahib / AFP / Getty Images: 40; Kin Cheung /
AP / Press Association Images: 28t; Marcel Antonisse / AFP / Getty Images: 12b; Mel Evans / AP / Press
Association Images: 13b; Pascal Rossignol / Reuters: 31; Paul Cooper / Rex Features: 25t; Petty Officer 3rd
Class Annie R. Berlin / U.S. Coast Guard : 7b; Photo courtesy of Northrop Grumman: 15c; Picture courtesy
Australian Customs and Border Protection Service: 28b, 35t, 35b; Pierre Verdy / AFP / Getty Images: 39; Press
Association / Tim Ockenden: 20cr; Reuters: 1, 25b; Reuters / Jason Reed: 30t; Reuters / Stringer Mexico: 19b;
Reuters / Stringer Philippines: 37t; Rex Features : 8b; Sajjad Hussain / AFP / Getty Images: 36b; Sipa Press /
Rex Features: 19t; Sipa Press / Rex Features: 36t; Stephane De Sakutin / AFP / Getty Images: 38b; STR New /
Reuters: 16t; Vario Images GmbH & Co.KG / Alamy: 41c; Wilhemsen / Rex Features: 30c.

A CIP catalogue record for this book is available from the British Library.

Dewey number: 363.2'85

ISBN: 978 0 7496 9353 4

Printed in China

Franklin Watts is a division of Hachette Children's Books, an Hachette UK company.
www.hachette.co.uk

Contents

Words highlighted in the text can be found in the glossary.

Keeping your country safe

Every country has borders. A border is the boundary around each country. Sometimes the border is marked by a high fence or other barrier, such as a river. Often the border is the sea coast around the country.

AF FACTS

The boundary between the USA and Canada is the world's longest un-defended border. It is 8,891 kilometres (km) long and crosses land and water.

Part of the United States/Mexican border. The US side is on the left.

Countries have laws to protect the people that live there. Laws help border officers to:

- Keep out illegal drugs
- Stop dangerous diseases from spreading
- Stop people who don't have permission to enter.

Many people work at the borders to keep their own country safe. Some inspect bags at airports. Others patrol the sea in ships or planes, looking for **smugglers** or anyone trying to enter the country illegally.

"Anti-terrorism is our primary mission but we are still focused on enforcement of immigration documents and illegal items." Arthur Gonzales, US Customs and Border Protection, Acting Port Director, El Paso, USA

Customs officers inspect bags.

Coastguards on patrol in New York harbour.

The protectors

There are many people working to protect our borders. They have different jobs that need special training and a range of skills.

Detection officers work at seaports, **land ports** and airports. They check everyone who enters the country. They look for people wanted by the authorities and people carrying illegal items, such as weapons. They also look for **illegal immigrants**.

Intelligence officers work behind the scenes. They gather information that assists in the detection of drugs and the arrest of smuggling gangs.

A detection officer carries out a search.

This X-ray shows people hiding in a truck. They are likely to be illegal immigrants.

Quarantine officers protect the country from dangerous diseases and pests. They check for people bringing in plants and seeds, as well as animals.

Coastguard officers patrol the sea. They watch for people trying to smuggle drugs or other goods by boat. They are also on the lookout for illegal immigrants.

ACTION STATS

The San Ysidro border crossing between Mexico and the USA (shown here) is the busiest in the world. An estimated 300,000 people use it each day.

MEXICO

Nada que declarar
Nothing to declare

Nada que declarar
Nothing to declare

Personal gear

Border officers across the world wear different uniforms. They also use different gear to do their jobs.

Detection officers usually wear lightweight clothing. In some countries they carry weapons. All officers have communications equipment to help them stay in contact with each other.

A detection officer checks a briefcase after it has been X-rayed.

"A typical day involves selecting traffic, examining vehicles or passengers' baggage, and interviewing passengers to see if they have prohibited or restricted goods." Andy Dawe, UK detection officer

AF FACTS

Smugglers use shoes with fake soles, hollowed-out religious books and bags with secret compartments to hide illegal items.

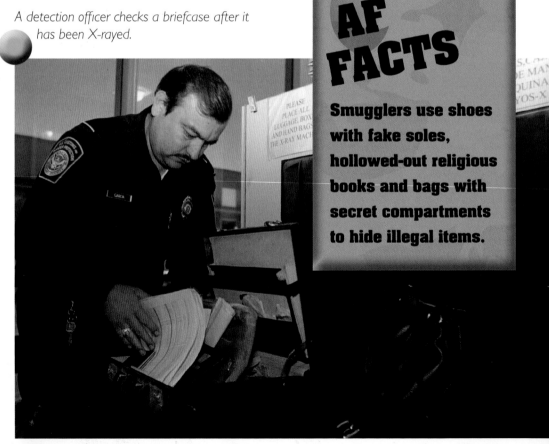

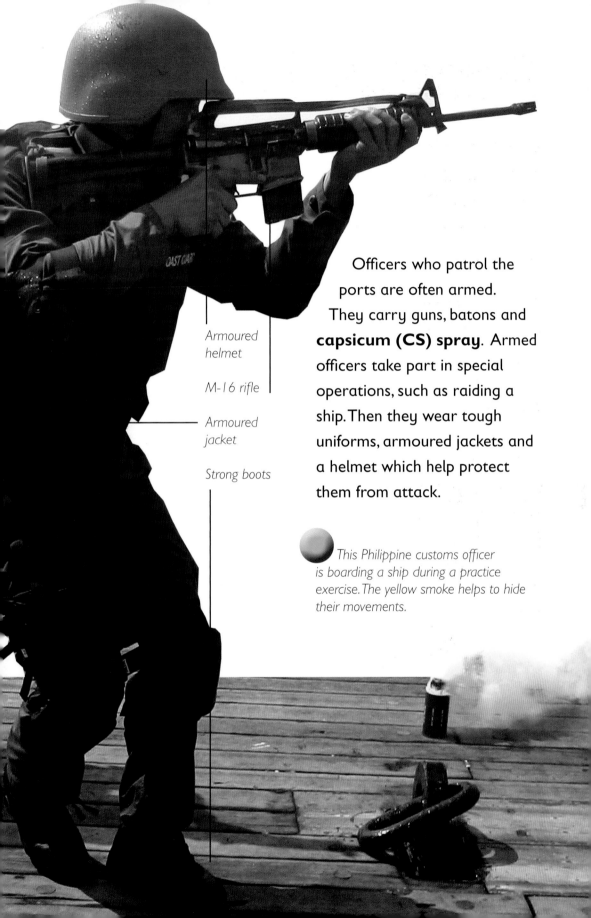

Armoured
helmet

M-16 rifle

Armoured
jacket

Strong boots

Officers who patrol the
ports are often armed.
They carry guns, batons and
capsicum (CS) spray. Armed
officers take part in special
operations, such as raiding a
ship. Then they wear tough
uniforms, armoured jackets and
a helmet which help protect
them from attack.

This Philippine customs officer
is boarding a ship during a practice
exercise. The yellow smoke helps to hide
their movements.

High-tech gear

Millions of people, vehicles and packages pass legally across borders every year. Customs officers need extra gear to check them carefully and quickly.

A US Customs and Border Protection (USCBP) officer checks for illegal items as bags pass through a scanner.

A passenger walks through a metal detector.

At airports, officers use scanners so they can see things inside bags. They scan to find hidden guns and other illegal items. They check passengers for metal objects, such as knives, when they pass through a metal detector.

This mobile truck X-ray machine is being used to scan containers at a seaport.

Customs officers check cargo containers using large X-ray machines. Containers are filled with goods, but smugglers sometimes hide drugs and other illegal items inside a container. The X-ray machine makes it easy for officers to see anything unusual hidden inside.

AF FACTS

Hand-held detectors can be used to find dangerous items, such as explosives. This machine (left) measures tiny chemicals in the air, and can be used to find bombs.

On the move

Officers patrol the air and sea in many different types of craft. Many countries cannot afford to buy all the equipment they need. This makes it harder to stop smugglers and terrorist activity.

ACTION STATS

The 'Midnight Express' intercept vessel (below) is the most powerful of its kind.

- **Top speed: 111 kph**
- **Range: 643 km**
- **Length: 12 metres (m)**
- **Power: 4 x 225 horsepower Mercury outboard motors**

Large coastguard ships are called cutters. They often carry one or two helicopters and use **radar** to search the water and the sky.

Smaller, faster boats are used to intercept smugglers when they attempt to bring illegal items into a country.

Planes can travel quickly looking for any suspicious activity, such as a boat travelling very quickly. They alert ground units who can move in to intercept them.

Two US Customs and Border Protection Midnight Express boats race to intercept a smuggler's speedboat.

Small jet aeroplanes are used to patrol coastal areas.

Coastguard helicopters have winches to lift people up quickly.

The Eagle Eye UAV is flown from cutters to assist in detection and search missions.

Helicopters cannot travel as far as planes, but they can fly and land in difficult places. Coastguard helicopters can be used to rescue people stranded at sea.

Unmanned Aerial Vehicles (UAVs) are planes that do not have a pilot. Officers control them from the ground. They can fly long distances, patrolling the border for many hours.

ACTION STATS

The Eagle Eye UAV can take-off vertically.
- **Top speed: 400 kph**
- **Range: 200 km**
- **Length: 5.5 m**
- **Power: Allison 250-C20 GT turboshaft engine**

Prohibited imports

Laws ban people from bringing some items into a country. These items **are called** prohibited imports. **Knives, guns and other weapons are usually prohibited imports because they are dangerous.**

These weapons were found hidden in a truck by Albanian border officers.

Many other items are not dangerous, but they are still prohibited. Illegal copies of console games, music, **counterfeit** money and films are all prohibited imports.

Smugglers hide prohibited items because they don't want border officers to find them. People can be fined or imprisoned if they are caught.

A customs officer in Jakarta, Indonesia shows how surfboards were used to smuggle illegal drugs.

Officers work behind the scenes using high-tech gear to battle the smugglers. For example, **UV** detectors (left) can be used to find things that are not visible to normal vision, such as chemicals.

AF FACTS

Officers use drug analysis kits to find out what a suspicious substance really is. They place a tiny amount of it into the kit. If the substance is an illegal drug, the kit detects it immediately.

This drug's test shows two pink tabs, which means the substance is not a drug.

MARIHUANA

Break left ampule
agitate one minute
Break middle ampule
wait for color
Break right ampule
color transfer
cover

Focus on:
Drug smugglers

Stopping smuggling across the borders is a full-time job for border officers. Drug smugglers are right at the top of their target list.

There are many illegal drugs, such as heroin, cocaine and ecstasy. The criminal gangs make money by selling the drugs. They smuggle different amounts, from a few grams to several tonnes.

Drugs gangs in parts of Africa use humans to transport small amounts of illegal drugs. They tape packets to their bodies underneath clothing. Others, called 'mules', are promised money if they swallow packets of drugs.

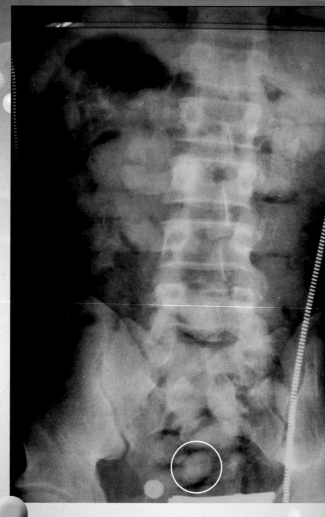

This X-ray shows the upper body of a drug mule. The lumpy areas (one is circled) are packets of drugs.

Arresting drugs smugglers and finding drugs takes a lot of work. Intelligence staff gather information about smuggling operations. Suspects can then be stopped as they try to smuggle items, and people in the gang can be arrested too.

Customs officers arrest two suspects at a shop in Mexico. Smuggling gangs usually have many members.

Detector dogs

A dog's sense of smell is thought to be a thousand times better than a human's. Border defence officers use trained dogs to detect drugs and other prohibited items such as explosives, plants, food and even cash.

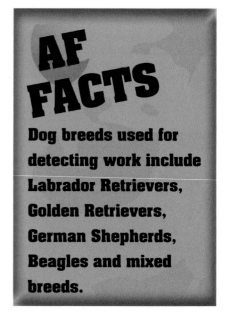

A detector dog and handler on duty at an airport.

A detector dog finds a packet during a training exercise at a warehouse.

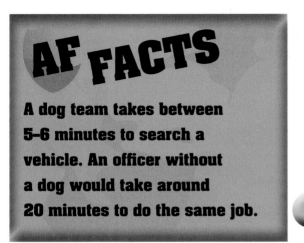

AF FACTS

A dog team takes between 5–6 minutes to search a vehicle. An officer without a dog would take around 20 minutes to do the same job.

This car is being checked at a land port.

Dogs are trained on agility courses to get them ready to work at airports, ports and other places. They climb over luggage and into cars – sniffing everything!

As soon as the dog detects a smell it has been trained to find, it stops and shows the handler where to look. The handlers reward the dog with a small treat.

This dog is taking part in an agility course as part of its training.

Airport security

A detection officer checks a passenger's passport as part of airport security.

Everyone who travels to another country by plane has to go through Customs. Officers look for prohibited items and also make sure passengers have paid duty, or tax, on legal items they bring in.

"The UK Border Agency is working hard to combat illegal immigration and Britain's border security has never been stronger."
David Holt, UK Border Agency

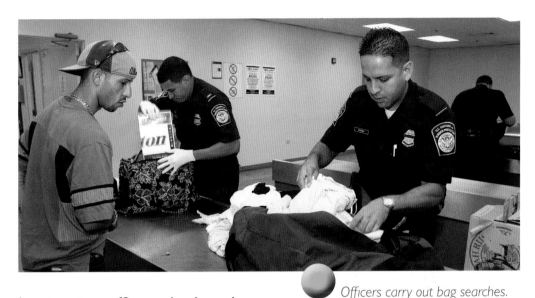

Officers carry out bag searches.

Immigration officers check each passenger's passport. This is a special document people need to enter and leave a country. They make sure that every passenger has the correct passport. Some people also need a visa; another document which allows people to work or stay for a set time.

Everyone has their bag checked by a scanner, but some are hand searched. Officers may do this if a passenger has come from a particular country, or is known to the authorities.

AF FACTS

The patterns in each person's eyes are different. Immigration officers can use an iris scanner to identify anyone who is logged in the system.

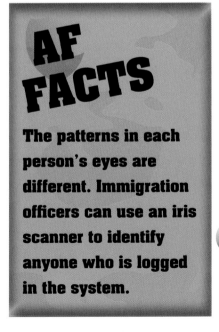
A passenger has his fingerprints scanned. This officer will also scan his iris to check his identity. Some countries keep records of iris scans.

Protecting the seaports

Every day, ships bring thousands of tonnes of goods into the seaports of the world. Most of these goods are carried in metal boxes called containers.

ACTION STATS

The busiest seaport in the USA is Los Angeles. The busiest port in the world (by tonnage) is Shanghai, China. The busiest passenger port in the world is Dover, UK.

This huge container ship is being unloaded at the port of Los Angeles, USA.

Customs officers patrol the ports. They check the goods that arrive. They search some containers for drugs or other smuggled items, but it is impossible to search them all.

A customs officer carries out a physical search of a container.

Customs officers also go on board ships and boats. They check that the sailors and passengers have the correct travel papers. They often climb around deep inside the ship, checking to see that there are no hidden items.

Turkish customs officers board a ship suspected of fuel smuggling.

Quarantine risks

Pests and disease can quickly spread from one country to another. To reduce the risk some items are placed under quarantine and are not allowed to be moved for a set period of time.

Quarantine, or biosecurity, officers are tasked with detecting dangerous plants or diseases that could accidentally come across the border. They check people entering the country for serious infectious diseases, such as tuberculosis (TB) or H1N1 swine flu.

AF FACTS

In Australia, plants can be quarantined if any of the following are found:
- **Diseases: Black Sigatoka, Citrus Canker, Citrus Greening Disease, Fusarium Wilt**
- **Pests: Citrus fruit borer, Exotic fruit flies, Mango pulp weevil, Sugarcane stem borer.**

A specially trained detector dog finds some fruit in a passenger's bag.

Officers wearing protective masks and gloves examine some flowers for pests.

Quarantine officers also inspect animals, farm goods, and fruit and vegetables that come into a country. Even spiderwebs or clumps of mud could accidentally carry a disease.

Quarantine officers clean or disinfect goods to make them safe. Sometimes they destroy goods to prevent disease risk or send them back to the country they came from.

Customs and Border Protection officers also work to stop wildlife smugglers. People sometimes bring in endangered animals **from other countries to sell as pets. They also bring in body parts.**

These elephants' tusks were found in a container in Hong Kong, China.

There is a long list of the world's endangered animals, known as the CITES list. Customs and Border Protection officers are on the lookout for anyone trying to bring these animals, or their body parts, into the country.

This man attempted to smuggle birds by hiding them in his pants!

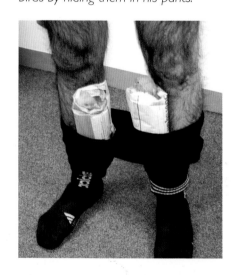

Smugglers sometimes try to sneak animals across borders in cruel and dangerous ways. Parrots and other endangered birds are often smuggled inside plastic tubes with very little air, and no food or water. Many of the birds die.

AF FACTS

Animal and plant smuggling is the second largest illegal trade after drugs. It is worth around £4 billion a year.

This chameleon was found during a search by German customs officers.

ACTION STATS

In 2005, Australian officers detected 545 incidents of wildlife smuggling at Australian airports.

People smuggling

Every day, people try to get into other countries without permission. These migrants want to escape from wars and other dangers in their own country. Other people want to move from a poor country to a rich country, looking for a better life.

These refugees were rescued in 2001 after their boat sank on its way to Australia.

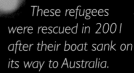

The Norwegian container ship Tampa rescued refugees in 2001. It was boarded by the Australian Navy.

Most countries are willing to accept small numbers of refugees and **asylum seekers**, but they still prefer to set a limit on how many people are allowed in.

"It remains our very strong determination not to allow this vessel or its occupants...to land in Australia." John Howard, former Prime Minister of Australia, speaking in 2001 about the Tampa refugees

Criminals smuggle groups of people into countries, such as Germany, Italy and the UK. They promise them jobs and a better life, but often they end up without any money and living in fear. Smugglers transport people in lorries, containers or in boats. Many people have died in these situations.

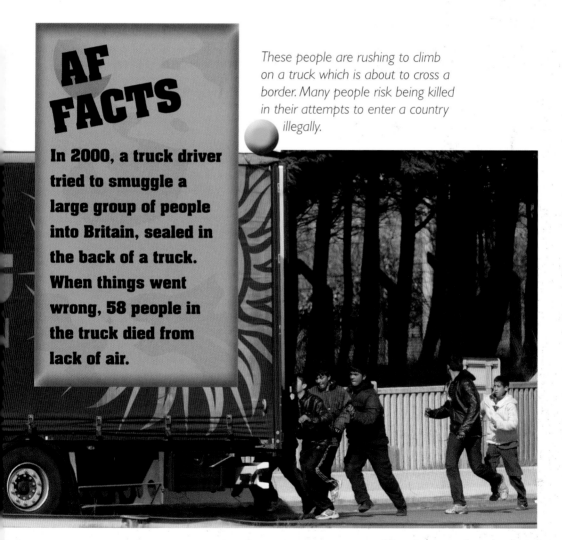

These people are rushing to climb on a truck which is about to cross a border. Many people risk being killed in their attempts to enter a country illegally.

Focus on:
US Customs and Border Protection

The **USA** is a large, wealthy country and attracts many illegal migrants from countries in South and Central America. US Customs and Border Protection (**USCBP**) work with authorities in Mexico to reduce the number of illegal people and items entering the **USA**.

Suspected illegal immigrants are stopped by USCBP officers on the US side of the US/Mexican border.

AF FACTS

There are around 7 million people living illegally in the USA, often working in low-paid jobs and living in poor housing.

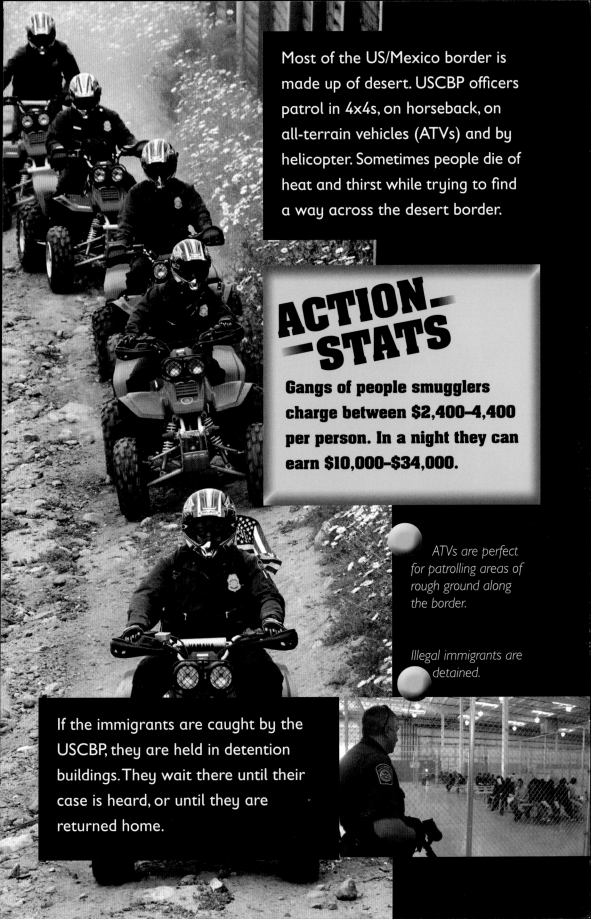

Most of the US/Mexico border is made up of desert. USCBP officers patrol in 4x4s, on horseback, on all-terrain vehicles (ATVs) and by helicopter. Sometimes people die of heat and thirst while trying to find a way across the desert border.

ACTION STATS

Gangs of people smugglers charge between $2,400–4,400 per person. In a night they can earn $10,000–$34,000.

ATVs are perfect for patrolling areas of rough ground along the border.

Illegal immigrants are detained.

If the immigrants are caught by the USCBP, they are held in detention buildings. They wait there until their case is heard, or until they are returned home.

Illegal workers

AF FACTS

In 2007, illegal workers in the United Arab Emirates (above) were given the chance to fly back home or to become legal migrants.

Every year, hundreds of thousands of people enter other countries illegally, hoping to find work. They usually come from poor countries, and want to earn more money. They get work in low-paid jobs, such as labourers on farms or on building sites, or as cooks and cleaners in restaurants.

German police and customs officers (Zoll) raid a farm suspected of using illegal immigrant workers.

People smugglers often take advantage of these illegal workers. They pay the workers very low wages. They charge them large amounts of money for 'protection'. The illegal workers usually live in fear of being caught and returned to their homeland.

German officers search for evidence of illegal immigrants, passports and emails.

Illegal fishing

Illegal fishing may not sound so serious, but it is a big business and affects a large number of countries. Experts believe the situation will get worse if fish stocks **fall further.**

Most countries have some part of their border on the sea coast. The actual border is around 19 km off the coast. The sea inside that area belongs to the country. Border defence officers try to stop large fishing boats from other countries coming to fish in their territory.

AF FACTS

Losses to illegal fishing worldwide in 2009 were about 11–26 million tonnes of fish. This doesn't include other sealife, such as turtles and dolphins, caught in illegal nets.

The Australian ACV Corio Bay stops a boat north of Darwin suspected of illegal fishing.

Staff on HMAS Warrnambool *prepare to stop a suspect vessel.*

Australia is the largest island country. Customs and Border Protection officers work with the Navy to patrol the sea. If they find boats fishing illegally in Australian waters, they can arrest the crew, destroy the boats, and remove the cargo of fish.

"We've got the local knowledge and the boats and the skill to get out there into the coastal environment where the illegal boats go and hide."
Dion Cooper, Djelk Ranger, contracted by Australian CBP to help patrol the Northern Territory Fisheries

An Australian CBP officer holds up shark fins found on an illegal fishing boat.

Fighting terrorism

A coastguard officer looks out across New York harbour.

Terrorists try to cause as much death and destruction as they can. Often terrorist attacks are carried out by people from other countries. Border defence officers are on the lookout for anyone who may be trying to come into the country to commit terrorist acts.

Terrorist groups often try to get into India from Afghanistan and Pakistan. The border area is rough and mountainous country. It is very difficult to patrol. Indian Border Security Force officers patrol the area. They use planes and helicopters, as well as 4X4s and ATVs.

Some borders, like this one between India and Pakistan, are heavily defended.

"We have caught two infiltrators trying to enter in the last two months." Major-General Tariq Yusuf, police chief of Iraq's Anbar province, which borders Syria

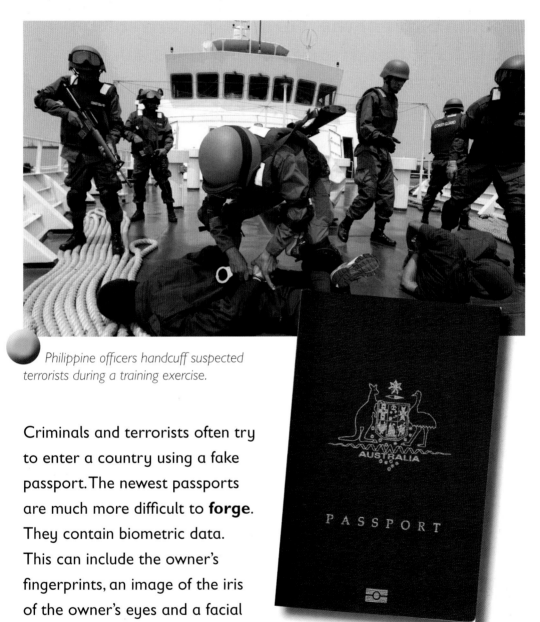

Philippine officers handcuff suspected terrorists during a training exercise.

Criminals and terrorists often try to enter a country using a fake passport. The newest passports are much more difficult to **forge**. They contain biometric data. This can include the owner's fingerprints, an image of the iris of the owner's eyes and a facial recognition image – all recorded on a microchip. No two people have exactly the same biometric data.

This Australian passport has a symbol at the bottom of the cover to show it has a microchip in it.

Piracy

In some parts of the world, there are still pirates. Pirates attack passing ships, such as large oil tankers, cruise ships and even smaller sailing boats. They usually hold them for ransom.

The pirates use modern weapons, such as automatic rifles and rocket-propelled grenades. They ride in small, fast boats.

 A French helicopter gunner looks out for pirates. He will shoot at the pirate boats and attempt to sink them (top right).

"The challenge that we have at border points is that [bandits] come from the same clan, and you find that sometimes it is hard to identify who is who." Kenya Defence spokesman Bogita Ongeri

Border defence and navy officers patrol parts of the sea where pirates might attack. Their job is to protect the ships. Naval ships from Japan, France, the USA and the UK all patrol dangerous areas, such as parts of the coast of Africa and China.

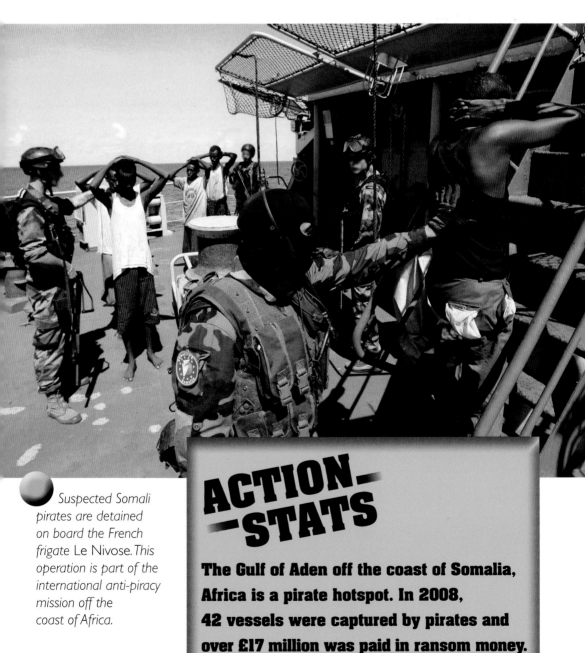

Suspected Somali pirates are detained on board the French frigate Le Nivose. This operation is part of the international anti-piracy mission off the coast of Africa.

ACTION-
-STATS

The Gulf of Aden off the coast of Somalia, Africa is a pirate hotspot. In 2008, 42 vessels were captured by pirates and over £17 million was paid in ransom money.

Fast facts

- There are about 11,000 US Customs and Border Protection agents. 89% work along the US/Mexico border. In contrast, there are about 980 agents working along the US-Canada border.

- A man was arrested in Los Angeles, USA in 2008 for smuggling three iguanas from Fiji. He hid them in his prosthetic leg, which he had hollowed out, before wearing it.

- In 2009, Spanish police seized £7 million in forged banknotes – the largest amount discovered to date.

- In 2009, the largest haul of heroin, valued at £8 million, was discovered at Heathrow Airport in the UK. It was hidden in holiday gifts sent from South Africa.

- Two pet dogs were used as drug mules when they had their stomachs stuffed with £126,000 worth of cocaine.

- In 2009, the UK Border Agency searched over 723,000 freight vehicles to check for illegal migrants, and stopped over 22,900 people attempting to cross the English Channel illegally.

Glossary

Asylum seeker – someone who is asking for the right to live in a foreign country.

Capsicum (CS) spray – a spray used to bring down a suspect as it makes the eyes stream and makes breathing difficult.

Counterfeit – an imitation of a product or document.

Endangered animals – species of animals who are so few in number that they are in danger of dying out.

Fish stocks – the numbers of particular types of fish, such as cod or halibut.

Forge – to make a false copy of an important document or signature.

Illegal immigrant – a person who has entered a country without permission, or is seeking to do the same.

Import – bring goods into a country.

Land port – a type of border station to control entry or departure of people and goods from a country across land.

Migrant – someone who moves to a different country, often searching for work.

Prohibited import – a good that it is illegal to bring into a country, including illegal drugs, weapons, fake goods or endangered animals.

Quarantine – a period of isolation for a person, animal or plant to prevent the spread of disease.

Radar – a device that tracks planes and ships using radio waves.

Ransom – usually a sum of money paid for the safe release of a hostage.

Smuggler – someone who, secretly and illegally, moves goods or people from one country to another.

UV (ultra violet) – a type of light ray invisible to the human eye.

Websites

www.cbp.gov/xp/cgov/border_security

This US Customs and Border Protection website features news videos of illegal goods seized, fact sheets and a huge image gallery.

www.customs.gov.au

Download factsheets about the Australian Customs and Border Protection Service from the media section, find out what Australia is doing to protect its borders, including all the latest detection technology.

www.kaiho.mlit.go.jp/e/pamphlet.pdf

Download this pdf about the Japan Coastguard which features maps, action images, case studies and everything you need to know about marine security.

www.ukba.homeoffice.gov.uk

Find out more about the work of the UK Border Agency, and the role that Customs plays.

www.daff.gov.au/aqis/quarantine/detector-dogs

Webpages of the Australian Quarantine and Inspection Service, highlighting the role of the detector dogs.

www.dhs.gov/files/counterterrorism.shtm

Find out more about counterterrorism operations on this website of the US Department of Homeland Security. It includes a link to the US Coastguard website.

http://sky1.sky.com/uk-border-force-exciting-new-series-takes-you-behind-the-scenes

Watch free episodes of Sky's exciting UK Border Force series which really bring the work of the UK Border Agency to life.

www.howstuffworks.com/airport-security.htm

Webpage from howstuffworks showing you all the stages of airport security and how it works, plus an image gallery.

www.panda.org

Use the search function on this official WWF website to find out more about animal smuggling, illegal fishing and CITES.

Index